Killer BIRDS

By Mignonne Gunasekara

Gareth Stevens
PUBLISHING

PREDATORS
ON THE PROWL

Please visit our website, www.garethstevens.com. For a free color catalog of all our high-quality books, call toll free 1-800-542-2595 or fax 1-877-542-2596.

Cataloging-in-Publication Data

Names: Gunasekara, Mignonne.
Title: Killer birds / Mignonne Gunasekara.
Description: New York : Gareth Stevens, 2022. | Series: Predators on the prowl | Includes glossary and index.
Identifiers: ISBN 9781538274194 (pbk.) | ISBN 9781538274217 (library bound) | ISBN 9781538274200 (6 pack) | ISBN 9781538274224 (ebook)
Subjects: LCSH: Birds of prey–Juvenile literature. | Predatory animals–Behavior–Juvenile literature.
Classification: LCC QL677.78 G858 2022 | DDC 598.9–dc23

© 2022 Booklife Publishing
This edition is published by arrangement with Booklife Publishing

Published in 2022 by
Gareth Stevens Publishing
29 E. 21st Street
New York, NY 10010

Written by: Mignonne Gunasekara
Edited by: Shalini Vallepur
Designed by: Amy Li

Photo Credits. All images courtesy of Shutterstock. With thanks to Getty Images, Thinkstock Photo and iStockphoto.

Recurring images – Ameena Matcha (old paper), teacept (header font), Alexey Pushkin (grunge texture), MrNoe (claw marks), Olga_C, Ografica (grunge shapes). Cover – Martin Dallaire, silky, p2–3 – Martin Dallaire, p4–5 – Ondrej Prosicky, Rudmer Zwerver, p6–7 – Sergey Uryadnikov, Alta Oosthuizen, p8–9 – fernando sanchez, Jesus Giraldo Gutierrez, p10–11 – MZPHOTO.CZ, Mark Bridger, TheRocky41, p12–13 – Geza Kurka Photos, Christopher P McLeod, p14–15 – Brian E Kushner, Chris Hill, Sekar B, p16–17 – Vadim Petrakov, Wang LiQiang, p18–19 – Harry Collins Photography, Studioimagen73, p20–21 – Jose Paulo Xavier Diogo, Milan Zygmunt, p22–23 – FloridaStock, Geza Kurka Photos, Harry Collins Photography, Mark Medcalf, Werner Baumgarten

All rights reserved. No part of this book may be reproduced in any form without permission in writing from the publisher, except by a reviewer.

Printed in the United States of America

CPSIA compliance information: Batch #CWGS22: For further information contact Gareth Stevens, New York, New York at 1-800-542-2595.

Find us on

CONTENTS

Page 4	Meet the Predators
Page 6	Red Kite
Page 8	Great Skua
Page 10	Barn Owl
Page 12	Common Kingfisher
Page 14	Bald Eagle
Page 16	Great White Pelican
Page 18	Peregrine Falcon
Page 20	Common Kestrel
Page 22	Spread Your Wings
Page 24	Glossary and Index

Words that look like <u>this</u> can be found in the glossary on page 24.

MEET THE PREDATORS

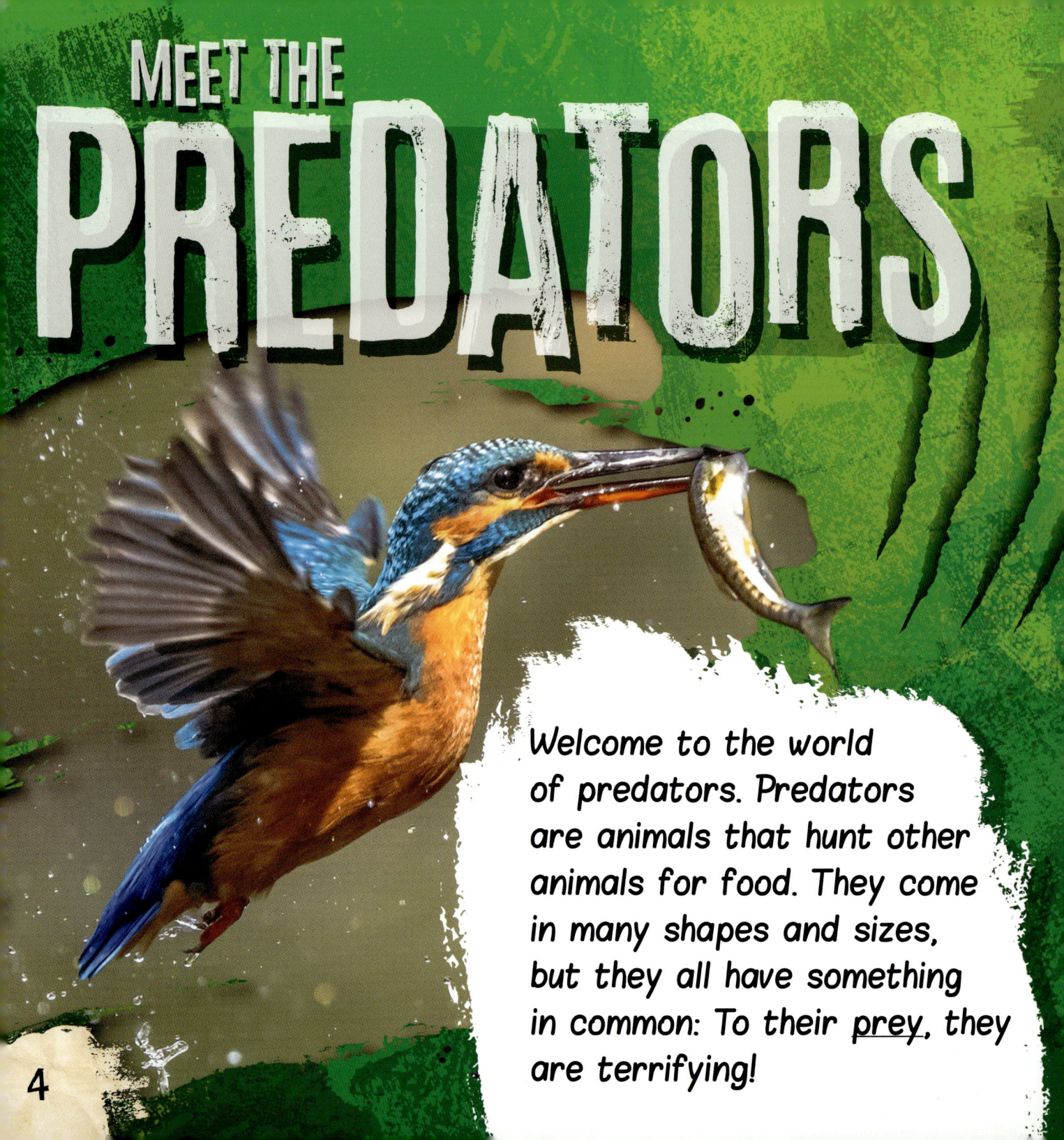

Welcome to the world of predators. Predators are animals that hunt other animals for food. They come in many shapes and sizes, but they all have something in common: To their prey, they are terrifying!

In this book, we will be looking at predators that are birds. They might look beautiful, but don't be fooled—they rule the skies as well as the roost.

A roost is where birds go to rest or sleep.

RED KITE

Red kites are mostly found in Europe and northwest Africa. In the past, the species nearly went <u>extinct</u>. Today, their numbers are growing.

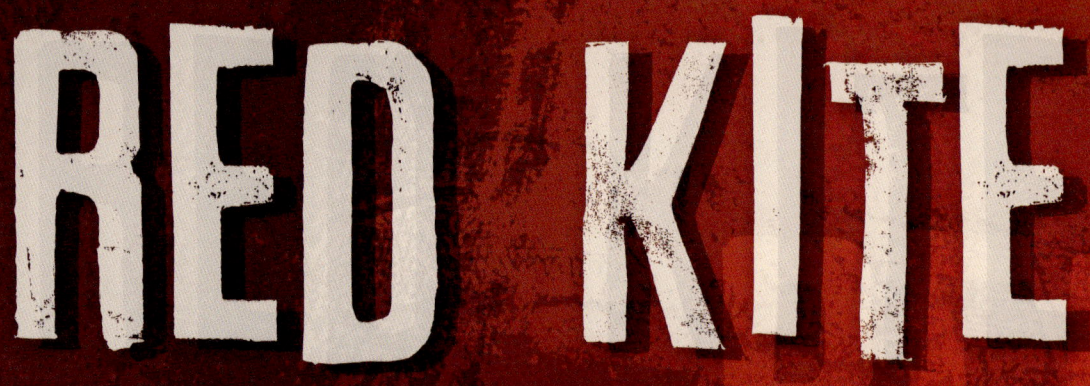

hooked beak

A species is a group of very similar animals that can have babies together.

Red kites are scavengers. They eat animals that are already dead, called <u>carrion</u>. They sometimes hunt for small animals, such as rabbits.

Fact File

<u>Habitat</u>: woodlands, open areas

<u>Weapons</u>: hooked beak

<u>Prey</u>: worms, small <u>mammals</u>, carrion

Red kites commonly eat whatever prey they can find.

GREAT SKUA

The great skua is known as a "pirate of the sea." This is because great skuas steal food from other birds.

The great skua is also known as the bonxie.

sharp beak

Great skuas eat smaller birds, such as puffins.

The great skua is a large seabird. It has been known to fly angrily at anyone that gets too close to its nest.

Fact File

Habitat: coasts, moors

Weapons: sharp beak, talons

Prey: fish, birds, carrion

BARN OWL

Barn owls have very good hearing to help them hunt at night. The shape of their face helps them to hear by sending sounds past their ears.

Barn owls can fly very quietly to sneak up on prey.

hooked beak

sharp talons

Barn owls <u>regurgitate</u> parts of prey that can't be broken down in the stomach, such as bones and fur. This matter is called a pellet.

Barn owls eat small mammals, such as voles and mice.

pellet

Fact File

Habitat: farmland, <u>grasslands</u>, <u>wetlands</u>, coasts

Weapons: good hearing, sharp talons

Prey: shrews, field voles, wood mice

COMMON KINGFISHER

These small, colorful birds can be found fishing near rivers and other slow-moving waters. They mostly hunt for small fish, but they also eat insects.

perch

Perches are places where birds can rest or take a good look around.

Common kingfishers hunt by sitting on perches near water, where prey is easy to spot. They dive into the water to catch prey and bring it back to their perch to eat.

fast flyer

The common kingfisher eats shrimp.

Fact File

Habitat: grasslands, wetlands

Weapons: speed

Prey: fish, insects, shrimp

BALD EAGLE

Bald eagles belong to a group of birds known as sea eagles. They have very good eyesight and can see prey from far away.

hooked beak

Bald eagles have sharp, hooked beaks to rip into food.

Bald eagles use their talons to grab fish out of the water. They also eat carrion and steal prey that other animals have killed.

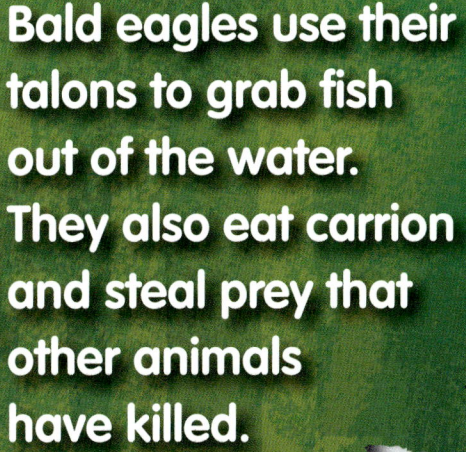

Bald eagles eat a lot of fish, such as salmon.

sharp talons

Fact File

Habitat: wetlands, grasslands

Weapons: good eyesight, talons, sharp beak

Prey: fish, small mammals, other birds

GREAT WHITE PELICAN

Pelicans are some of the largest birds on Earth. They are known for the stretchy pouches under their <u>bills</u>, which they use to scoop fish out of the water.

Pelicans have webbed feet to help them swim.

large bill

throat pouch

webbed feet

16

Great white pelicans usually fish in groups. They swim together and push the fish into one area, then scoop them up to eat.

Pelicans can fly for long distances to look for food.

Fact File

Habitat: wetlands

Weapons: bill, hunting in groups

Prey: fish

PEREGRINE FALCON

Peregrine falcons can be found everywhere, from cliffs by the sea to tall buildings in cities. A peregrine falcon's main prey is birds.

Peregrine falcons hunt prey such as pigeons.

pointed wings

talons

They grab prey out of the air with their talons.

Peregrine falcons hunt by diving at their prey while flying. They can reach speeds of over 185 miles (300 km) per hour while diving!

Fact File

Habitat: most places except Antarctica

Weapons: talons, speed

Prey: mostly birds, bats

COMMON KESTREL

Hovering makes it easier for the common kestrel to see and catch their prey.

sharp talons

Common kestrels have an interesting way of hunting. They can stay in one place in the air while flying. This is called hovering.

sharp beak

Common kestrels can be found in many habitats. They eat small mammals such as voles, mice, and shrews. In towns and cities, common kestrels may find it easier to eat birds than mammals.

Common kestrels mainly eat voles. They sometimes eat insects and worms.

Fact File

Habitat: farmland, grasslands, towns and cities

Weapons: talons, good eyesight

Prey: small mammals, small birds, insects, worms

SPREAD YOUR WINGS

Congratulations, you met the predators! Weren't they fierce? Let's see them stretch their wings and fly!

Which bird has the biggest wingspan?

Red Kite

6 feet (1.8 m)

9.6 inches (25 cm)

Common Kingfisher

GLOSSARY

bill	a bird's beak
carrion	rotting parts of dead animals
extinct	no longer existing
grassland	an area of land where grass is the main plant that grows
habitat	the natural home in which animals, plants, and other living things live
mammal	an animal that is warm-blooded, has a backbone, and makes milk to feed its babies
moor	an open area where rough grass grows
prey	animals that are hunted by other animals for food
regurgitate	to bring up food that has been swallowed into and out of the mouth
talons	claws, especially those belonging to birds of prey
wetland	an area of land that is very wet or covered in water

INDEX

beaks 6–10, 14–15, 21
carrion 7, 9, 15
diving 13, 19
eyesight 14–15, 21
fish 9, 12–13, 15–17
flying 9–10, 13, 17, 19–20, 22
habitats 7, 9, 11, 13, 15, 17, 19, 21
hunting 4, 7, 10, 12–13, 17–20

insects 12–13, 21
perches 12–13
prey 4, 7, 9–21
stealing 8, 15
talons 9–11, 15, 18–21
voles 11, 21
worms 7, 21